Adapting the Soccer Religion in Nigeria

Alex Ndukwe

Copyright © 2020 Alex Ndukwe

All rights reserved

This book or any portion thereof may not be reproduced or used without the express written permission of the publisher except for the use of brief quotations in a book review

First printing, 2020

Printed in the united states of America

ISBN: 978-1-79482-885-8

Dedication

This book is dedicated to Mr Abubakar Suleiman, CEO, Sterling bank plc for impacting positively in his immediate environment and Nigeria with his exemplary Leadership qualities.

Forward

'Soccer Religion' my terminology that was derived from the reactions and attitude of people involved with this sport during a soccer match. The bottom line is striving to excel, the components that make up the ecosystem are Players, coaching crew and Fans. These components are connected no matter what transpires.

Love was a common factor that connected these components and this is responsible for the oneness of the fans when supporting their teams, factors like ethnicism, religion are swept under the carpet and you will see them embrace or hug themselves when the ball finds its way into the opponents net with resounding joy.

Love for our nation is what we need for us to obey the laws of the land, ensure we serve our people that we represent with all our hearts, come out with policies that impact the lives of the common man on the street.

Patriotism is love for our nation without limitations and this will make things to work in our society. The lessons learnt from the 'Soccer Religion' should impact individuals, corporate entities, Government across the board and our society will be a better place.

Alex Ndukwe

TABLE OF CONTENTS

	Page
Analysis of Soccer Religion	7 - 15

Chapter 1
Copycat Syndrome   16 - 28

Chapter 2
National Interest not Negotiable   29 - 44

Chapter 3
A Collective effort   45 - 63

Chapter 4
Closing the Poverty Gap   64 - 104

The Soccer Religion

Soccer, the most popular sports in the world and as a little child I watched our national team participate in continental, Regional, world competitions. I remember Cot devoir 84 nations cup, semi-final match we played against Egypt, radio commentaries gave detailed description of events on the pitch, I could recall that we were two goals down, the reaction was like eagles cannot fly today and I corrected our friend, it's just some minutes in the first half, I believe green eagles will fly and many of us continued to follow proceedings with that game.

Julius Agohwa reduced the tally, Ernest Okonkwo of blessed memory screamed, it's a goal, Julius ensured he followed the ball to the net, in the gathering were people from different tribes, Christians, Muslims and there was one unifying factor, the round leather kicked around on the pitch. When the equaliser came in the second half, most people embraced themselves and Joy filled the whole atmosphere. This match resulted in a penalty shoot-out, the doubting Thomas's that left returned to follow the match and it ended 10 – 9 in our favour, tiny groups of Four were formed, with love the just concluded match was analysed, don't forget every soccer fan in Nigeria is a coach.

I want to draw your attention to 1985 FIFA U-17 world cup that was hosted by the Peoples Republic of China, 50% of the team hailed from Bendel state now Edo state, it was evident that selection process was on merit and the ethnicity of the players didn't matter to anyone. The trophy was won and every Nigerian walked ten feet tall in Beijing on this fateful day.

A greatest footballing nation like brazil worship the God of Soccer, Apologies to our religious Leaders, recall what happened in brazil 2014 when the host team was trashed by Germany, the stadium turned to a graveside, fans left the arena, most fans that kept faith in their national team wept like babies. You can see the passion for their country even in defeat.

In 1990 during the execution of Ogoni-9, Ken Saro-wiwa and his kinsmen, Nations Cup final was in progress in Algeria, the CNN journalist asked his respondent about the reaction of Nigerians, he reminded him that Nations cup final was currently been watched and no one has time for the issue at hand until after the match.

The supporters club also a very important component when our national team is in action, songs that spurs, inspire, energize our team and song rendition speaks of turn of events, when Super eagles is down, you will hear, 'he's a miracle-working God....., He delivered Paul and Silas, will surely deliver us', when it's a barren draw you will hear, 'All we are saying give us one goal' when eagles refuses to fly, the will be booed and the message is clear, we don't celebrate mediocrity but excellence.

Our national team was ranked no 5 before the 1994 world cup in the USA and this crop of players remained the best in the history of Nigerian Soccer, it took a technical coach like Arrigo Sachi of Italy to unseat them in the second round, he simply instructed that Daniel amokachi and Emmanuel Amunike to be unplugged in that match and this paved way for their two strikes that made us lose that game.

Can you remember the 1996 Dream team, we were three goals down and my friend told me this match is one-sided, we kept the faith, as usual, the story changed before the end of regulation time, it was Kanu Nwankwo that equalized and also got a winner. Bebeto was a shadow of himself as he wept like a baby.

The lessons from these are that we can be great as a nation, the footballers are skilful, resilient, hardworking and most of them risk their career should injury occur, this might end their professional career, but they put the national interest first. Fans provide support, the behavioural pattern is worth emulating, there is no religious inclination, hatred etc. rather all you will see is unity, love, all they can see is their nation coming out tops. We need to take a cue from this and adapt it to our lives.

Soccer is the most popular sport in Brazil. Football quickly became a passion for Brazilians, who often refer to their country as "o País do Futebol" ("the country of football"). Over 10,000 Brazilians play professionally around the world.

("Natal Brazil". Natal Brazil. September 29, 2006.)

Soccer has a major effect on Brazilian culture. It is the favourite pastime of youngsters playing football on the streets and indoor Futebol de Salão fields. The World Cup draws Brazilians together, with people skipping work to view the national team play, or employers setting up places for employees to watch. The General Elections are usually held in the same year as the World Cup, and critics argue that political parties try to take advantage of the nationalistic surge created by football and bring it into politics. Former Brazilian footballers are often elected to legislative positions. One unique aspect of Soccer in Brazil is the importance of the Brazilian State

Championships. For much of the early development of the game in Brazil, the nation's size and the lack of rapid transport made national competitions unfeasible, so the competition centred on state tournaments and inter-state competitions like the Torneio Rio-São Paulo. Nowadays, however, there is a growing tendency of the devaluation of the importance of such championships as continental and national competitions have grown in relevance since the early 1990s.

Worldwide soccer is the most popular sports that have the power to bring people together, has a unifying force of bonding and racial discrimination in Advanced countries is the only negative part as successful black players are abused because of their colour, Let us look at the positive side of the game. Patriotism is very evident as most people around the world could display pain when their team is losing with attached emotions.

This book was triggered by the consistent high figures attached to recurrent expenditures, 2020 budget has about 7 trillion Naira and other heads are not adequately provided for, I believe in the Leadership of my country and at the same time we need to look for ways to seek reforms that will improve our lots in Nigeria, my book on 'Nigeria can be great', the truth was told, we cannot afford to lose hope there is light at the end of the tunnel, we need to adopt the 'Soccer religion' as a way of life and we will see positive transformation.

The following are the lessons we must learn from the soccer religion, we need to visualize the attitude of the players and the fans, these we can adapt to our way of life in Nigeria, they are as follows:

1) Players put in their energy and they ensure that victory is assured, we could call it patriotism

2) When sports Administration is not working and funds are not available, in some cases the players continue to feature in tournaments

without complaint, this incidence occurred at Brazil Olympics, a foreign-based player had to pay the bills from his pocket.

3) The players travel from all part of the world to represent their country

4) The players risk their professional career, they could get injured or lose they're live like Samuel okwaraji.

5) The Players bring glory to their motherland

6) Fans are not left out; they unite no matter their background and render support to their national team

7) Fans are very important when considering the ecosystem of soccer Soccer is referred to as a religion because a universal language is spoken that is understood, the movement of the round leather and when it

gets to the back of the net people scream, rejoice, jubilant and sit at the edge of their seats when the opponents attempt to score. The religion has come to stay, and we need to emulate it in our national lives and polity.

Chapter 1

Copycat Syndrome

'The Asian giant is making big strides toward that goal. Copying other people's technology may be a thing of the past in China. Since 2011, the Asian nation has led the table of the countries filing the largest number of patents.'

Once upon a time, china once copied technologies and produced their product at that time products originated from Japan and you hear traders tell you that this is Taiwan and today they have become the heaven for production of consumer goods, united states companies have factories there now, copycat has since ended.

Our democratic dispensation has evolved for over 20 years and as a nation, we still move circles, the gains are not felt on the streets, the time has come for us to access the system that we run and adopt a homegrown democratic system.

Like the United States, Brazil, and India, Nigeria is structured as a federation, a structure it inherited from its British colonial rulers. It has thirty-six states, one federal territory, and 774 municipalities (plus Abuja). Yet power resides in the central government, which controls most of the country's revenues and resources. A 2005 constitutional review attempted to address the controversy over revenue sharing and the tenure of the president and state governors but ended without progress after the introduction of an amendment that was widely seen as a political move to extend Obasanjo's time in office by two years.

('Nigeria's Creaky Political System', Council on Foreign Relation, Stephanie Hanson, April 12 2007)

We have heard Nigerians clamour for restructuring, a shift from federalism to Regional governance and as a nation, we must take adequate decisions in this light but we must be ready to have a critical look at available data at our disposal. These are not my expectation, in my opinion, political Jobbers are only interested in their fortune and there is no iota of patriotism in this at all and I must ask this question which I consider very vital, 'What have we achieved with constitutional conference organised by various administration?', these documents have gathered dust and taxpayers money are wasted in this direction and we continue to encourage waste of resources in our polity that lacks patriotism.

An extract of the constitutional conference consummated during Goodluck ebele Jonathan regime, Main recommendations from the National Conference:

• Scrapping the current system of 774 local authorities - this is intended to save money and reduce corruption. States would be able to set up their local systems

• Creation of 18 new states - equally spread around the country. Also suggested that states wishing to merge can do so if certain conditions met

• Revenue allocation - proposes reducing the share of national income going to the federal government and increasing share for the states

- A modified presidential system of government that combines the presidential and parliamentary systems of government. The president should pick the vice-president from the legislature

- Power should be shared and rotated at all levels of government. The presidency should rotate between north and south and among the six geo-political zones of the country. Likewise, the governorship post should rotate among the three senatorial zones in each state

We need to discuss the resolutions from this conference, I cannot understand the wisdom of scrapping the Local governments, can be described as unrealistic, how do we get governance to people in the rural area, how much do we intend to save from this exercise? Though we might argue that LGA is underdeveloped since independence, which is correct but we need to understand that State government sit on the funds and refuse to release such funds to the LGA, recently FG has decided to disburse allocations directly to the LGA's and NFIU ensuring the funds are not embezzled by the LGA officials. This is a laudable initiative that will ensure development springs in these environments.

'The federal government has ordered that federal allocations to LGAs be disbursed directly to their respective bank accounts starting from June 2019. According to him, the directive means that LGAs allocations will go to their bank without going through their governors as was the case with Joint Account System. It's my candid belief that the new order will indeed bring the desired development at the grassroots as well as allow the spread of dividends of democracy to the electorate. Another plus to the order is that it will help checkmate most of our state governors, who have blatantly refused to conduct local government elections. The governors have continued to use caretaker chairmen to siphon LGAs funds. I am happy that the new rules also state that LGAs without elected chairmen will not get an allocation from the federation account. Many of the states without elected chairmen should hurriedly conduct their election so as not to be left out from their subventions, this is indeed a blessing in disguise, Mwolwus stated.''

('PDP Chieftain lauds FG's new directive on LG funds', Pulse, News Agency of Nigeria, 13th May 2019)

When the states are allowed to create their structures, this is an avenue to encourage corruption, state governments will embezzle funds meant for these rural people and its not a perfect idea I must confess.

Creating 18 new states in Nigeria is not very important as most of the states in existence are not viable in terms of revenue generation and these states would become a Liability to the Federal government, political jobbers nursing ambition of taking care of their belly's sponsored this agenda at the conference and it should be ignored and should never be re-echoed.

Revenue Allocation, more income to the states than federal, the formula is already indicated in our constitution, oil-producing states receive more allocation, the issue is that the revenue generated from crude export continue to dip and the cake has suddenly become very small and there is nothing to share except crumbs, this should awaken creativity, revival of internally generated revenue, take a deep look at ways in which state government can generate revenue, it might even be tourism which remains an untapped area.

An example is Mambila plateau, a potential tourism site that has remained untapped in Taraba state, surprisingly there is no good access road to this location and the onus lies on the state government to make this area a tourist attraction that will yield revenue and Leadership should come with vision that cannot be distorted but bring about the desired improvements.

The modified presidential system, we run American system of governance and apart from the fact that it is not cost-effective it is alien to our culture and cannot bring out the best out of our potential Leaders, the norm of a Leader stepping down for the other which encourages mediocrity. We don't need to run a multiple party state, rather we should adopt one-party system, everyone will belong to the same party, the primary election would now become an election that will decide who becomes the president-elect, this will enable participation of candidates and they would have to reel out visions if elected into office. This would enable us to eliminate unnecessary electoral expenditure incurred by the umpire, INEC.

The single-party system fosters unity and there is no rivalry experienced like multiple party system and it suddenly becomes a do or die affair, Afterall we are after improvements of our country there should be bonding where we are united with common purpose devoid of any bitterness.

The homegrown democracy should ensure that cost of governance is reduced to the barest minimum and we avoid wastes, why do we need the Red and green chambers, parliament should be reduced to one and have a representative from each ward, this implies that the house will have 119 members and this will make governance very efficient and cost would be significantly reduced compared to the system we run today.

Interestingly we had organized system before colonialism, history students will recall that empires like Mali, Borno had existed and is a proof that in Africa we are not disorganized, then we need to understand that copying American presidential system cannot take us to the promised land, it only encourages waste of resources thus our homegrown democracy should be enthroned.

The constitution must be amended to cater for the reforms, it is not cast in stone, the stakeholders should imbibe the soccer religion, which was described at the beginning of this book, patriotism is the bedrock of this universal religion practised worldwide. There is a need to push for the reforms of our democracy and it should not end up been passed and nothing happens. Our Leaders in power should understand that no one can be greater than our nation, we must move for the amendment of the constitution.

Political office holders should understand reasons why they are elected to office, they need to consider themselves as servants to the people and must be seen as protecting their interest. Ethnic associations like Arewa forum, Ndigbo, Independent People of Biafra and Afenifere, OPC, Oduduwa peoples congress should be discontinued and discouraged in the spirit of adopting the Soccer religion. These associations would not help us as a nation rather an agent of retrogression and indication of decay in our nation.

The IPOB that is clamouring for an independent state should stop deceiving themselves because this will not improve the lot of an average Igbo man, rather the issues of discrimination will persist within them, this happened during the existence of Odimegwu Ojukwu led Biafra government, the South-South indigenes were dwarfed in his government, some Igbo tribes consider themselves as real Igbos and others as counterfeit, this would not lead to any improvement and must be discouraged.

The Soccer religion, there is no iota of ethnicity, there is unity across the board, and this should reflect in our lives. We need to co-exist as people that are united and with the focus of building a great nation.

Power should be shared and rotated at all levels. The soccer religion, selection of players is done by merit, the best players are selected to strengthen the squad, though we might argue that quota system comes into play, in most cases coaches prove difficult when the best players are at his disposal. Now suggestions that power should be rotated at the six geo-political zones for the presidency. We need to note that this will enthrone mediocrity, what happens when there is no competent person in a political zone. I strongly suggest that capable leaders should be elected no matter where they come from. The interest of the electorate should be the candidate that has a laudable manifesto, vision and developmental agenda that will improve our nation.

The electorate should be able to assess at the end of the tenure, should such a leader come for re-election, the performance would determine whether he/she should return to power. Our democratic institution should evolve to this extent, I am sure some school of thought would argue that these assertions can only take place when some certain challenges are resolved like the INEC must remain independent and not influenced by the government of the day, electoral processes are improved and devoid of rigging and thuggery.

The resolutions were made during the constitutional conference organized by President Goodluck administration, I decided to make use of the recommendation made and it is evident that the political jobbers are the ones making this demands and if another conference is organized the same resolution will be made, this is a clear indication that we need to discontinue such conferences and carry out referendum as practised in the advanced countries, the people should speak their mind and not the politicians representing them and the crux of the matter is that our people are not well represented.

Chapter 2

National Interest not Negotiable

Nigerians are transactional in nature and this is a fact from my experience, we need to shift from such behavioural pattern in our society, I recall a pastor recounting his experience when he was posted to Israel at the Nigerian embassy, his close friend put a call across and asked him if he could assist him to get some contracts, the pastor wondered what kind of request is this.

Citizens of Nigeria have thrown national interest to the dogs and no one cares, there must be a change of attitude in this direction and I want to commend President Muhammadu Buhari, his traits have brought some remarkable improvements to our nation, a two time head of state that has served Nigeria in various capacities and at the age of 77, he is still making laudable impact.

According to my friend Olaoluwa, 'he should be considered rich but a poor man by choice', this assertion I considered a very strong statement that describes our Leader, his fight against corruption indicates that he has put national interest paramount before any other thing, one of the high point was the conviction of Orji Uzor Kalu by EFCC, despite his defection to APC and immunity as a lawmaker in the red chambers.

Policies his government has reeled out has revamped agriculture, now Nigeria has stopped the importation of Rice with CBN intervention for farmers, though it is a gradual approach that will affect other food produced locally, ban on importation of dairy products would affect these farmers positively as the big players like Dano, Wamco has signed MOU's with the farmers in Kaduna state.

The border closure has blocked smuggling of Rice and other products to our country, initially when Nigeria signed an Mou on free trade among the African countries at AU most people felt that our country is not producing goods and soon we will become a dumping ground and this action has proved otherwise as we now see the positive effects during the closure, a poultry farmer in the south has experienced surge in demand for chicken from 4,000 to 12,000 birds per day, he's unable to meet up an everyone can see that our economy will become stronger with this initiative.

The government has shown us that national interest must be above our interest and we must fall in line as a citizen of Nigeria. What should be in our hearts is Abraham Lincoln's assertion, this time we substitute Nigeria for united states, 'What you can do for Nigeria and not what Nigeria can do for you'.

We need to take a critical assessment of ourselves can we substantiate the claim that National interest is paramount in our hearts than our interest. Then this implies that we will shun nepotism, ethnicism, corruption, violence, thuggery, fraud etc. I quite agree that we have experienced decay in our society as regards morals and ethical standards. Today in Nigeria the rich is more respected than people endowed with intellectual properties, no one cares about the source of wealth. There is a need to change our mindset. In the religious circles, the rich are accorded more respect and given more responsibilities than the intellect.

Let me put it this way, what do we consider national interest?

'National Interest' is a key concept in International Relations. All the nations are always engaged in the process of fulfilling or securing the goals of their national interests. The foreign policy of each nation is formulated based on its national interest and it is always at work for securing its goals. It is a universally accepted right of each state to secure its national interests. A state always tries to justify its actions based on its national interest. The behaviour of a state is always conditioned and governed by its national interests. Hence we need to know the meaning and content of National Interest.

Our Actions, perceptions, behavioural patterns, determine whether we are undermining our national interest, a recruited thug during election by politician that refuses to be used to unleash mayhem at the polls could be described to have national interest in his heart because his actions will affect the process negatively and the international observers are watching and reports will be given to the whole world.

Nationalism is an ideology and movement that promotes the interests of a nation (as in a group of people) especially intending to gain and maintain the nation's sovereignty (self-governance) over its homeland. Nationalism holds that each nation should govern itself, free from outside interference (self-determination), that a nation is a natural and ideal basis for a polity, and that the nation is the only rightful source of political power (popular sovereignty). It further aims to build and maintain a single national identity—based on shared social characteristics such as culture, language, religion, politics, and belief in a shared singular history and to promote national unity or solidarity. Nationalism, therefore, seeks to preserve and foster a nation's traditional culture, and cultural revivals have been associated with nationalist movements. It also encourages pride in national achievements and is closely linked to patriotism.

Every citizen must possess this trait and it will rub on our nation positively, one of our problems is waste of scarce resources, the bottom line is that as public office holders accountability is vital, we must ensure that waste is eliminated, when we embark on laudable projects it must not turn moribund after a while, this implies that value has not been added, we will take an example.

In 2007 we heard of investments by the governor of cross river state called TINAPA, a 60billion Naira investment going down the drain.

Since April 2, 2007, when the project was inaugurated, it has (slowly) become moribund. For an N55.88bn ($470m) project that was designed to be a world-class destination for tourists and people of business concerns from all over the world, the attention it drew was almost second to none.

The project, conceived by the Cross River State government, under the then leadership of Donald Duke, was expected to generate employment opportunities and be a veritable source of revenue for the state and the country at large. But, nine years after its take-off, all these projected results have remained expectations and many still wonder what could have happened to such a project. Another failed initiative that would have generated revenue and attracted patronage within and west African subregion. Dear reader let us review this as a case study.

TINAPA TOPOLOGY

Tinapa is a mixed-use development sitting on 265 hectares of land, comprising a business wing and leisure resort wing. It is located within the Tinapa Free Zone and Resort and adjacent to the Calabar Port and the Calabar Free Trade Zone. The location was to ensure easy access to the port and to take direct delivery of manufactured products from the CFTZ. It's cited in the outskirts of Calabar on a land that was previously being used for rubber plantation in Adiabo community in Odukpani Local Government Area of the state.

Conceptualised as a world-class trading and resort hub, the first of its kind in Africa, it comprises a wide range of complementary components, which include trade and distribution, accommodation, conferencing, entertainment, leisure, food and beverage, cultural and educational, agritourism and ecotourism facilities. Notably, its financial viability was to be driven primarily by import, export and trading activities in addition to services offered by the leisure and tourism components of the project. The trade wing of Tinapa consists of four emporiums of 10,000 square metres each, 100 retail outlets, 53 shops ranging from 150 square metres upwards, parking lot for about 4,000 cars, etc. The leisure section, on the other hand, comprises the magnificent Lakeside Hotel, a 242-room (inclusive of 59 executive suites) luxurious hotel, Tinapa water parks with scintillating slides and swimming pools, said to be the largest in Africa, casino, cinema, Studio Tinapa, conceived to be the centre of Nollywood entertainment in Nigeria. These facilities have remained idle.

Trade wing, which was meant to be the major attraction in the centre, is now bereft of activities. In fact, to say that several business owners who still manage to run their businesses there are deeply frustrated because there is no patronage. Even the movie studio that gulped a whopping N4.3bn and was expected to further boost the nation's

Nollywood industry has not contributed anything till date.

Financial institutions like the First Bank, United Bank for Africa, Ecobank that opened for anticipated business opportunities have since closed down out of frustration and lack of patronage, telecommunication companies (MTN, Globacom and Etisalat) that had shops in the trade wing have had to shut down their businesses largely due to lack of patronage.

What are the challenges?

Tinapa was not in operation for the first two years after its inauguration due to inoperative guidelines and framework, and the delay was one that economists say could have dampened the enthusiasm of some would-be investors. But following the intervention of the then Managing Director of the Tinapa Free Zone and Resort, Chief Bassey Ndem, who initiated moves to make the set guidelines operational, the hub experienced a sudden boom.

Between 2009 and 2012 two out of the four emporiums were fully occupied with wholesale and retail businesses, while 42 out of the 53 shops were also put into good commercial use. But the boom was short-lived as it slowly snowballed into its current state. Many business owners left the premises one after the other based on what they described as unfavourable government policies, high operating cost (including exorbitant rent), unwholesome activities of the regulators and clash between the operators and regulators.

In 2012 Customs officials started disturbing customers, Purchases in the threshold of N30,000, attracted duties payment and It became inconvenient for customers and many of them stopped patronising businesses in that facility, investors could not sell their products, it didn't make any sense to continue running businesses, goods became too expensive this led to businesses shutting down.

Meanwhile, a provision in the incentives and concession agreement as seen on Tinapa website, says "Persons who purchase goods up to a maximum of N50,000 or its equivalent within Tinapa Free Zone and Resort, in respect of which valid receipts from approved enterprises operating within the zone, have been issued, shall be entitled to import such goods into the Nigerian Customs Territory, duty-free and all customs and other licensing requirements that apply to goods imported into Nigeria Customs Territory from other countries shall not apply to such goods."

Also, apart from the fact that the project is located at the outskirts, which could discourage willing customers, the refusal of the Federal Government to complete the dredging of the Calabar waterways to enable vessels bringing goods to access the site has discouraged importation of goods. While the port would have fast-tracked import and export from the zone, dredging of the sea is still facing slow progress due to hitches between contractors and the Nigerian Port Authorities. Thus, investors who would have shipped their goods could have opted out of their plans. The alternative for those who are resilient would be to make use of Lagos seaport (about 752km away) or the Onne Port in Rivers State which is about 215km away.

Findings, however, showed that trade zones are usually sited around seaports to facilitate import and export and the absence of it can render the entire project inefficient. The Lagos Free Trade Zone under construction, a port is coming with it. Look at the Onne Oil and Gas Free Trade Zone in Rivers State, the Onne port is there. So, until the Calabar Sea is dredged, and the port is put to use, independent of other administrative issues, Tinapa might continue to depreciate without meaningful impact. Tinapa even has an advantage because it can import and retail its products, unlike the Calabar Free Trade Zone that is mainly for manufacturing.

A projected three million visitors expected to carry out business activities in the facility yearly with about N100,000 projected income per person, it was estimated that about N300bn would be realised annually. But, sadly, this is far from reality. As of 2009, the facility attracted only about 500 visitors daily and between then and now, many businesses have closed while patronage has reduced drastically.

After Donald duke's administration, we have had two administrations and none of them has looked into this Tinapa issue, debts accrued from this investment is just been serviced and reasonable income is not realised, can we see that there is no continuity concerning old and new administration of cross river state, this kind of problem is experienced everywhere in Nigeria. From this short story, the initiator of this project did not do his homework before executing this project, the stakeholders would have been involved and actively engaged to ensure that the dredging of the Calabar waterways was executed without delay. The framework that will allow the environment to become a tax-free zone should have been concluded, it's not heard that such a zone will be invaded by Nigerian customs.

National interest is paramount, waste should not be entertained and the government of the day in cross river state should take responsibilities and fix this problem and make this venture effective to achieve its set goals of 300-billion-naira income that is projected, Jobs will be created directly and indirectly.

Government Administrations are only interested to show that they are working by carrying out New projects, we should look beyond the just building, managing such infrastructure should be sole responsibilities of the newly installed administration, continuity is very essential and when this is not done, values created by past administrations are destroyed.

Ajaokuta steel rolling mill is another failed project that has undergone series of concessions and no solution is in sight, we would recall that steel is an important component for production all over the world, government of the day should look for strategies to fix this mill, engaging the likes of Price water house, enerst & young etc for a road map would not be a bad idea, this facility must work and add value to our economy. It has suddenly become a shame that no administration can fix this problem. A gubernatorial aspirant in Kogi state addressed the house, I'm not sure of her claims concerning the mill at the red chamber. There is a need to stop all this drama and take the bull by the horn.

Chapter 3

A Collective effort

We have discussed the Government concerning expectations not met and the people been governed must take responsibilities, our roles and involvement will make the policies meaningful and workable.

Though I have mentioned our roles in nation-building in my book titled, 'Nigeria can be great', this was discussed at the surface and this chapter will take an inadept approach concerning our attitude concerning the subject matter.

Our mindset as citizens of Nigeria must change, do we love our country?

When it comes to love of country this takes the form of ideological transactions, the kind that fuels partisan rigidity: I'm gonna sell you on my idea about how things work (the economy, states' rights, gender, religion, military interventions, etc.) and if you buy it that means we are both patriots. Fromm took our understanding of love even further, well beyond even just a critique of transactional arrangements. He also described an understanding of love that transcends those arrangements. In the psychology of love, he charted, the point of view and experience of the other matters as much as one's own, not more and not less. You do things not to get back but because of a genuine connection to the other. One gives because giving is a genuine expression of self, and one receives with the same empathic spirit of genuine engagement. It is like art, an expression of self. And once again, patriotism comes down to duty and service where what you do to be patriotic needs to be an expression of who you genuinely are.

('The Art Of Loving Your Country', Forbes media, Todd Essig, 2019)

The love every citizen must exhibit is an essential component for the development of our nation, this is just beyond patriotism, our attitude portrays this trait and this is beyond waving the national flag, wearing jerseys of super eagles etc. let us look at the following issues:

1) Taste for foreign goods

2) Evading Taxes

3) Engaging in Anti-development activities

4) Tool for violence

Taste for foreign goods

Ours is a country with citizens who mostly have an unquenchable desire for foreign-made things. To the upper class, the elites, buy them locally made goods and you have insulted their 'pedigree'. To the 89 million poor people in Nigeria, the ability to purchase foreign-made things is a huge sign that they have 'made it' and are really 'punishing poverty'

(The excessive taste for foreign-made goods: a fault in our star, Lifestyle Nigeria, Adeola Oladipupo, November 13 2018)

Most of us are guilty of this and we hurt our economy by patronising foreign brands and our local industries continue to struggle, this should not be a one-sided discourse, Our local firms should improve on their quality as well. Improved patronage is assured, despite the policies of government restricting Foreign exchange for the importers. If truly you love our country embrace locally produced goods and services, some Nigerians dry clean their suits overseas and the claim here is that the suit is too expensive, our local patronage will create employment. Automobiles are not left out, let us buy locally produced cars, Some of the cars we invest our monies on the whites rarely buy them and we must stop buying such cars.

I don't know why we invest money buying a G-wagon, I here it's prestigious but you are boosting the economy of the foreign land at the detriment of our own, it's high time we curtail our taste. In the United Kingdom taxes on luxurious cars are very high and its high time government introduce heavy taxation on such products to discourage the use.

Welcome to Nigeria where people queue to buy Ghana garri because it is mixed with brown sugar. In this part of the world, people scramble to purchase Ghana-sealed soup because of the ingredients in it. This is where school uniforms are imported from China and other countries by some big-name Nigerian private schools just to show off.

We need to curtail our taste and stop buying foreign goods and this is the only way to boost our economy by embracing local content.

2) **Evading Taxes**

Tax evasion is an illegal activity in which a person or entity deliberately avoids paying a true tax liability. Those caught evading taxes are generally subject to criminal charges and substantial penalties.

As individuals we must ensure we pay our tax, though most people have their PAYE taxes deducted from source, there are still other personal transactions that are taxable and we must ensure there is no evasion of any sort when this is done you deprive the government funds meant for development.

Most individuals own businesses and they must ensure that taxes are paid, though we see the government introduce taxes like stamp duty for deposits in bank accounts, payments with POS etc. we must understand that advanced countries depend on taxation and in the Advanced countries impose a luxury tax on luxurious goods purchased. Though we need to ensure as good citizens we don't evade tax.

In economics, luxury goods are referred to as Veblen goods, which are defined as goods for which demand increases as price increases. Since taxes increase the price of a good, the effect of luxury taxes may be an increased demand for certain goods that are luxury. In general, however, since a luxury good has a high-income elasticity of demand, both the income effect and substitution effect will decrease demand sharply as the tax rises.

3) **Engaging in Anti-development activities**

The question in our hearts should be the real meaning of

anti-development? These are actions that undermine the efforts of the government, vandalization of infrastructure, theft of public funds etc. the love of one's country should make us desist from these actions. We are taking a cue from the soccer religion. Can we remember our national pledge and I want to remind us, it's as follows:

"I pledge to Nigeria my country, to be faithful, loyal and honest. To serve Nigeria will all my strength, to defend her unity, uphold her honour and glory, so help me God."

We need to understand this pledge, it's a commitment we are making and our action should be beyond reciting this pledge, the portion that concerns our discussion is 'uphold her honour and glory', how can we uphold her honour and glory is by ensuring that negative actions should be avoided as much as possible, corruption has eaten deep into our fabric and public funds that would have been used to develop our country is stolen and poverty inflicted on our society and we hear derogatory assertions are made by some advanced countries, calling our motherland the capital of poverty in the world, this is unacceptable primarily because of our actions and we are not able to uphold the 'honour and glory' of our nation.

In most democracies in the world it is not impossible to have protest and disagreement with policies of government, this should not be a license to destroy infrastructures and the cost of replacement is very huge and it might become difficult to replace and afterwards, we will feel the pain, let us put our country first as this action will jeopardise development in our country.

"It's hard to love this country right now. I doubt if the relatives of the 150 plus souls that so needlessly perished in that Dana plane crash are feeling any 'allegiance' right now. It is bad enough when it is a freak accident, but for a disaster of such magnitude to have been set off by such gross negligence as is being reported is unacceptable and hard if not impossible to forgive."

('I pledge to Nigeria my country…..', vanguard, June 8, 2012, Tiola)

This reference is disturbing because an accident occurred and the writer claims it's hard to love the country now, this is how most of us have missed it, even if someone is not doing his/her job, this should not make us hate our nation, we need to manage our emotions and address issues appropriately, nothing should make us substitute our love for Nigeria. Emotional imbalance is responsible for our negative actions, there is no need to join the bandwagon and dishonour our motherland. No matter the number of passports you carry there is no place like home.

One of the ways we can 'uphold her honour and glory' is to be creative and ensure we add value to our society, we need to understand that our little quota can bring positive improvements to our nation.

Corporate bodies are not left out in the quest of adding value to the society, we are looking beyond corporate social responsibility which is very common, shared values have taken over in the world today.

"The quarrying industry adds a great deal of value to society, but the questions that need to be asked are 'where?' and 'how?'. Without answers to these questions, there is little point assuming that this is the case. Society's use of quarried products and the provision of local employment are often cited as good examples of value-adding activities, but rarely are these quantified and, as a result, they are often regarded more as folklore than fact. Unless companies know precisely what their products do and where their employees come from, the answers to these questions can be little more than guesswork. It is not acceptable to be anywhere other than in full understanding of the balance of payments between the business and society."

('Adding Value To Society', AggNet publication, Dr Miles Watkins, director of group environmental and corporate social responsibility, Aggregate Industries UK Ltd)

How can our corporate bodies add value to our society, there is no limit to these but we must understand that impacts can be made in our rural community and we need to look at a more sustainable programme that will impact on individuals and our country at large. I want to give examples and I discussed it with my friend olaoluwa some days ago, 'I simply asked him if he had ever witnessed the processing of cassava to produce Garri', according to our deliberation I told him the pains the rural dwellers undergo for days to produce this commodity and I witnessed it and felt so bad.

One of the ways our corporate bodies can impact on this rural dweller that are predominantly farmers is by installing cassava processing plant in these communities, collaborate with these communities and come to terms with them or look for a frontline farmer that will take responsibility of managing this facility in that locality, proceeds generated will be used to repay for the cost of this equipment, other farmers can bring their produce for processing on a first come first serve basis for a little fee. Commercial banks should buy into this idea, it's a way of adding value.

Other challenges posed by some of these communities is lack of access roads from their communities to major cities, the local government should be active by ensuring PPP initiative is used based on BOT (Build Operate and Transfer) even if tolls are introduced on the portion of the roads constructed to recoup the cost of construction. Road construction firms should add value in this area.

There are enormous ways of adding value to the society and we should visualise this act as a noble way of adding value to these communities and our nation because they serve as a food basket for our nation, issues of processing, storage, preservation should not be a challenge. There is an enormous waste of produced food in these communities.

We need to commend the founder of Dangote Industries, Alhaji Aliko Dangote for the ongoing refinery project adjudged to be the biggest in the whole world concerning its capacity, though we agree it's a business enterprise geared at making profits and we must look beyond this and recognize the fact that the firm will soon add value. This investment implies that it will create employment directly and indirectly. The virus that has ravaged our economy, 'Petroleum Subsidy' will be laid to rest for good and this waste can be converted to use for other purposes, I don't want to bore you with figures it's not necessary.

The processing facilities for the Dangote refinery include a crude distillation unit (CDU) and associated facilities, mild hydrocracking (MHC) unit, a residual fluid catalytic cracking (RFCC) unit, a naphtha hydrotreater, and a gasoline hydrodesulfurization (HDS) unit as well as alkylation units. The refinery complex will also house sulphur recovery and hydrogen generation facilities and a polypropylene unit. Comprising two steam methane reformer (SMR) units, the hydrogen generation facility will generate 200,000Nm^3/h of hydrogen and steam to produce sulphur-free fuels. The other processing units at the refinery include the STRATCO® alkylation unit, the MECS® sulphuric acid regeneration (SAR) unit, the MECS® DynaWave® sulphur recovery unit, and the BELCO® EDV® fluid catalytic cracking unit. The refinery is designed to produce up to 50 million litres of gasoline and 15 million litres of diesel a day.

('Dangote Refinery, Lagos', NS Energy Report)

5) **Tool for violence during Election**

The youths are the ready tools used by some politicians to perpetrate violence during elections, I want to advise the youths to desist from this act and they should look beyond the incentives they are promised. When the electoral process is disrupted you indirectly destroy your future.

However, commitments to peace around election time by political parties and candidates isn't enough to bring stability. In 2011, about 800 were killed in post-election attacks on minorities across northern cities. In 2015 about 100 deaths were recorded. While the commitment promised in peace accords is important, the structural drivers of violence must also be tackled. Two such drivers are particularly important.

One is the state control of productive resources and domination of economic life in Nigeria, which creates the perception of state office as an easy avenue for accumulating wealth. The other is the politicisation of security and law enforcement institutions and questions about their neutrality. The 1999 Constitution, the Land Use Act and the Petroleum Act give complete ownership and control of the oil and gas sector to the state. The sector, managed by the Nigerian National Petroleum Corporation (NNPC) through joint ventures with foreign firms, is the mainstay of the economy. It accounts for more than 50% of government revenue, placing considerable resources at the state's disposal. The federal government is the sole receiver, divider and dispenser of oil revenue based on a complex formula between itself and the 36 states.

As such, much of the country's economic activity is politically controlled and many private sector players depend on political patronage. Public works and procurement, whether federal or state, are major sources of business and employment and are bankrolled with oil money. The ability to win contracts depends on one's political connections. For many political candidates, politics has become the only way to improve their lot. For others, it is a matter of personal prestige or simply being in control of people and resources. For those seeking economic gain, winning elections is the endgame. It is a common belief that candidates – and their financial backers – invest heavily in elections to harvest returns on their 'investments' when they win the stakes become high and the signing of peace accords, although important to reduce the political temperature, are not enough to forestall violence.

The youths are not actively engaged in any vocation, some that are graduates being unemployed and these politicians take advantage of them, one of the ways of curbing this problem is by providing vocational training that will make our youths productive and ensuring that they are useful to themselves and society.

Cooperate bodies are actively involved in creating enabling environments that can engage our youths and equip them with skills that will make them self-reliant.

"Leading Nigerian commercial bank and Africa's most agile the company, Sterling Bank Plc has announced its investment in the the global multi-billion-dollar software engineering sector in

partnership with Decagon Institute. Speaking at a press conference recently, Khafil Animashaun, Head, Strategy & Innovation at Sterling Bank, disclosed that Decagon's mission of training 5,000 software engineers, creating 30,000 jobs, and generating about $1 billion in export revenue over the next five years aligns with the bank's vision of

improving the H.E.A.R.T (Health, Education, Agriculture, Renewable Energy and Transport) sectors. The partnership with Decagon

Institute is part of the bank's intervention in the education sector through investment in ideas and execution of projects that will advance it. Sterling is working with Decagon to identify and transform young talented Nigerians into world-class software developers at scale.

We are certain our investment will bridge the software development the talent shortage in the country's fast-growing technology ecosystem while also positioning our youth to compete in the fast-paced global software engineering market, Animashaun added."

("Sterling Bank invests in billion-Dollar non-oil revenue sector", TechPoint Africa, 14 August 2018)

Our youths should be engaged, and such programmes Organised Would add values to these youths and keep them engaged. Such programmes should be taken to our rural areas where youths in their productive age are not employed, this will help to curb electoral violence.

Chapter 4

Closing the poverty gap

"Nigeria has overtaken India as the country with the largest number of people living in extreme poverty, with an estimated 87 million Nigerians, or around half of the country's population, thought to be living on less than $1.90 a day. The findings, based on a projection by the World Poverty Clock and compiled by Brookings Institute, show that more than 643 million people across the world live in extreme poverty, with Africans accounting for about two-thirds of the total number. In Nigeria, as with other countries on the continent, that figure is projected to rise. "By the end of 2018 in Africa as a whole, there will probably be about 3.2 million more people living in extreme poverty than there are today," the researchers write. Despite being the largest oil producer in Africa, Nigeria has struggled to translate its resource wealth into rising living standards."

("Nigeria overtakes India in extreme poverty ranking", CNN, Bukola Adebayo, June 26 2018)

Before we proceed on further discussions let us look at the paper delivered by Muhammad Sani Abdullahi, Commissioner (sub-national Minister), Ministry of Budget and National Planning of Nigeria at the world economic forum, the extracts are as follows:

Extreme poverty statistics have always been controversial. Many countries and experts disagree with the way it is measured in monetary terms – the World Bank's $1.90 earnings-per-day benchmark. But no matter what the arguments might be, at the root of poverty lies the deprivation of people's access to necessities such as food, healthcare and sanitation, education and assets. And the evidence - including from India - shows that solving these issues generally lifts populations out of extreme poverty.

As global attention turns towards my country, Nigeria, here are three ways that concerned stakeholders and policymakers can assist in the efforts to achieve the first of the Sustainable Development Goals (SDGs) - to end poverty.

1) . **Invest in girls' education**

Nigeria is home to over 10 million out-of-school children, around half of whom are girls - and it is hardly coincidental that the country with the world's highest number of out-of-school children is home to the highest number of people living in extreme poverty. Two-thirds of this population is concentrated in Nigeria's highly populated north-west and north-eastern regions, both of which have been ravaged by the terror group, Boko Haram, resulting in an educational emergency affecting about 2.8 million children.

The 2018 Global Multidimensional Poverty Index (MPI) of the Oxford Poverty and Human Development Initiative best presents this picture. The poorest parts of Nigeria had the worst education indicators (school attendance and years of schooling) and these constitute the biggest percentage contribution to the MPI, followed by nutrition and child mortality – all issues that affect women the most. Educating girls is proven to have both economic returns and intergenerational impact. For Nigeria to improve on this front, it must increase its investment in education.

My state, Kaduna - where I oversee the organization with the mandate of planning and fiscal resource allocation - has consistently increased its education budget over the past decade. As a result, enrolment figures have doubled from 1.1 million students in 2015 to 2.1 million students in school today. The state now ranks the highest in the northern region, recording the highest score in the senior school certificate examinations.

2. Invest in health and wellbeing

Increased investment in healthcare is linked to economic growth, and consequently to reducing poverty. Nigeria is battling with several crushing health indicators including malaria, tuberculosis and infant and maternal mortality, all of which have a sweeping impact on productivity.

To end poverty, we must harness the demographic dividends through investment in health, education and livelihoods - especially for our young people. In remarks he made on October 2017, International Day for the Eradication of Poverty, the late Professor Babatunde Osotimehin - former executive secretary of the United Nations Population Fund - argued that "when countries' age structures change favourably, meaning that they have more people of working age than dependents, they can see a boost to development, known as a demographic dividend, provided that they empower, educate and employ their young people."

He was right. Sub-Saharan African countries - the last frontiers of poverty in the world - are witnessing explosive population growth, and the region is projected to grow by about 51% over the next three decades. The UN projects that Nigeria will have an estimated 398 million people by 2050, making it the third-largest country in the world.

Lower population growth is not an automatic panacea for poverty. Rather, an educated, healthy and resilient youth population, as has been the case in China, is the best catalyst for growth. However, an absence of planning or allocation of insufficient resources towards harnessing this bulging population could spell doom.

3. **Expand economic opportunities and embrace technology**

Ending poverty in Nigeria will entail improving the country's economic productivity and opportunities for its citizens. This will mean investing in human capital potential and creating jobs for women and young people, increasing financial access and opportunities these groups in rural communities, and advancing technological innovation.

Nigeria ranks 152 out of 157 countries on the World Bank's Human Capital Index. One of the low-hanging fruits would be to embrace educational reforms that focus on developing new skills through robust and well-funded technical and vocational education and training programmes for those millions of Nigerians outside the formal school system, or who possess only primary education. Unlocking private-sector partnerships through incentives and social impact bonds as well as boosting entrepreneurial ecosystems (with a strong emphasis on apprenticeships) are key ways the government can help to spur growth, as has been proven in other countries.

Also - and notwithstanding its limitations - access to microfinance has been proven to reduce poverty around the world. While there are valid arguments for the use of grants and other social safety pay-outs to people living in poverty, it is important to bring people into the financial system as this could help governments better plan and integrate services for the poorest of the poor.

Let us look at the paper delivered and x-ray the points mentioned:

10 million out-of-school children, around half of whom are girls, this is the first point mentioned and it's pertinent to note that the region worst hit is Northwest and Northeast, I would not want to trade blame at all because attempts have been made to curb this problem, past Administration built schools for Almajeri's in the North, today these

schools have been scrapped and this might be as a result of inability to fund them. One issue we must deal with is the 'early girl marriage' been practised, it should discourage, and National Orientation Agency should handle it by providing a platform to discuss with parents of these children. It cannot be enforced because it is a sensitive issue that has the religious inclination. Emir Lamido Sanusi has been championing the education of girls in Kano and he has been under heavy criticism.

I remember vividly that Rabiu Kwankwaso former governor of Kano state converted Daula hotel to a girl's secondary school, this is a positive step in the right direction but how many parents will release their girls to attend the school. One expedient thing is to re-orientate the parents and make them see the reasons why their children should attend schools.

"The Emir said an educated girl would grow to become a woman who can effectively take care of the home and thus ensure a healthy society. The Emir of Kano, Muhammadu Sanusi II has advocated for the rights of the girl-child to education in the Northern part of the country. Sanusi while speaking at the flag-off of the second phase of the immunization campaign in Ajingi Local Government Area of Kano State on Wednesday, November 22, said the girl-child education is the only key to development.

Sanusi added that women and children formed 70 % of the Nigeria population and that taking proper care of the percentage would lead to building a better nation that is capable of attaining all its intended developmental goals."

("Emir of Kano advocates for girl-child education in the North", Pulse, Bayo Wahab, 24th November 2017)

Other issues are the poor funding of education, our yearly budget is so insignificant, it has been an age-long problem in our society, it would be a surprise to discover that some communities don't have a conducive environment for learning, FGN should make education top priority. We have the potential of excelling in the world, in my book, 'Nigeria can be great', the world university chart, 3 Nigerian universities were listed and no African country was listed, covenant university – 601, University of Ibadan – 1,001, University of Nigeria Nsukka – 1004. This is an indication that more schools can be listed with better ratting.

Every stakeholder must take responsibility and the love for our nation must be exhibited while lasting solutions are proffered. I want to challenge the state governments to embark on free education for the primary and secondary level, this would support the initiative of ensuring poor parents can send their children to school.

The second point in this paper, Increased investment in healthcare is linked to economic growth, and consequently to reducing poverty. Nigeria is battling with many crushing health indicators including malaria, tuberculosis and infant and maternal mortality, all of which have a sweeping impact on productivity.

Nigeria has made serious of efforts to ensure that our hospitals are equipped, we must do more and most importantly use technology to leverage the shortage of medical personnel by adopting the Internet of things(IoT) , the process was fully discussed in my book, 'Internet of things(IoT): A Challenge for Nigeria', I want a policy reeled out to ban Medical tourism and this will make our stakeholders take our hospital very serious and ensure they are equipped with the state of the art equipment.

The government should be ready to allocate more resources to this sector and make it viable especially at the rural area.

A boost to development, known as a demographic dividend, as long as the health care yields desired results, this means that the workforce that is properly trained will be available to the economy and not children and this would eradicate poverty.

investing in human capital potential and creating jobs for women and young people, empowerments of the adult population, making them productive and self-sufficient. The human capital index is very poor, and this implies that there is no adequate training for human capital in Nigeria.

Though we have NGO's take the initiative to train unemployed graduates or Job seekers, this cannot be enough, more must be done to raise our position and ensure that employable citizen can have prerequisite skills that will enable them to be self-employed. All hands must be on deck to ensure that the deplorable position is improved.

The stakeholders in Nigerian economy should be creative, take a look at the North and see the roadmap for eradicating poverty, we should be ready to Add value in our immediate communities, while we wait for big brother FGN, let's identify contributions that we need to make.

In my book, 'Nigeria can be great', I mentioned and discussed approach, it does not matter how little, if we have all-hands-on-deck we will see that it sums up and smile will be put on someone's face.

Everyone is engaged in corporate social responsibility which is not a bad idea, let us look beyond given people a plate of rice, rather teach the fellow how to fish and stop providing free fish, a time will come the fellow becomes self-reliant. I want to salute prince ebeano supermarket, this organisation constructed a 3.5 kilometres road from Gudu to Lokogoma in FCT. They have added immense value to this community, and this will not only help customer visit the ebeano mall, but it will have a positive impact on economic activity.

The government should allow corporation adding value use the efforts rendered to negotiate their tax, even if it means for them to enjoy a rebate. Each time I want to shop I go to that mall because of what he has done concerning road construction.

In this writeup our focus is creativity, consumers pay a lot of charges, especially commercial bank customers and this is counterproductive as it will dent the cashless policy of CBN. Why charge stamp duty for POS transactions we are pleased with CBN's swift reaction and reduction of bank charges.

The reviewed charges for banking services are contained in the new "Guide to Charges by Banks, Other Financial and Non-bank Financial Institutions," which now supersedes the 2017 version.

The CBN said the new charges were "arrived at after extensive consultations with stakeholders and the action is expected to enhance flexibility, transparency, and competition in the Nigerian banking industry."

The guide stipulates a penalty of N2million per infraction or as may be determined by the CBN as a guard against excess, unapproved or arbitrary charges by banks and other financial institutions. Besides, failure by any bank to comply with the

CBN's directive in respect of any infraction shall also attract a further penalty of N2million daily or as may be determined by the apex bank, until the directive is complied with.

To emphasise the seriousness of the new rule, the Director of Corporate Communications Department, CBN, Isaac Okorafor, said the banks had been directed to henceforth log every complaint received from their customers into the Consumer Complaints Management System (CCMS).

Additionally, they are to generate a unique reference code for each complaint lodged, which must be given to the customer.

"Failure to log and provide the code to the customer amounts to a breach and is sanctionable with a penalty of N1million per breach," he said.

According to him, "this is the time financial services providers and their customers alike have to acquaint themselves with the provisions of the guide and be guided accordingly."

Specifically, for cards linked to a savings account, the maintenance fee has been reduced to a maximum of N50 per quarter from N50 per month amounting to only N200 per annum instead of N600.

(Why we cut bank charges, by CBN, The Guardian, Mathias Okwe, 23 December 2019, page 1)

The government should encourage the private sector to provide infrastructure in their immediate communities and afterwards a coupon for tax rebate handed over to them not less than amount expended. Dangote is attempting to use cement to tar roads instead of extremely expensive coal tar.

A new concrete road is now open to traffic in Nigeria's Kogi State. This is of note as the new 24km road is the now the country's longest to be made from concrete The new road was built in a joint venture partnership between Nigerian firm Dangote Construction and Brazilian company Andrade Gutierrez. The new road connects Kabba with Obajana. Part of the Dangote Group, Dangote Construction was well placed to carry out the work as it operates its Obajana Cement production facility, at Obajana.

This new road could well set a precedent for road construction in Nigeria. The country does have a high level of seasonal rainfall, which can result in rapid wear and tear for asphalt roads. Vehicles in Nigeria are also frequently overloaded, further increasing wear rates for asphalt types of roads. But concrete roads may cope better with the seasonal rainfall and may also provide greater resistance to vehicle overloading.

Drainage is a key issue for Nigerian road construction also, as the country's seasonal tropical rainfall can result in large volumes of rainwater being deposited in a small area in a comparatively short period. The performance of this stretch of road in Kogi State is likely to be watched with great interest by the road authorities in various states across the country, as well as by the Federal Government in Abuja.

Dangote explained that it opted for this method of construction as using a slipform paver offers a productive method for road building, while also delivering a uniform structure. With a cement facility close at hand, the firm says it was able to monitor and maintain concrete quality to the necessary specifications and ensure a homogenous mix was supplied to the paver. Monitoring the paver's operation also ensured that the necessary road profile could be achieved, according to Dangote.

The construction work for the 24km stretch of road took six months, with the road lying on a base comprising a compacted laterite filling and 150mm crushed stone. The road has been constructed on top of the base structure, using a Wirtgen SP 500 slip former to pave the lanes in each direction of travel. This has required the construction of 3.65m wide by 200mm thick slabs in either direction, featuring 12mm diameter tie bars. Wirtgen's local dealer was able to deliver training to the road construction crew from Dangote and Andrade Gutierrez, to make sure the personnel were able to make the best use of the SP 500 meanwhile.

(Nigeria has built a major road link from concrete, World Highways July August 2016,)

Shared Value Initiative

the Shared Value Initiative was created in 2012 to drive the adoption and implementation of shared value strategies by organizations around the world, we will look at an article published so that readers can understand these initiatives since the world is moving away from CSR. Article published by FSG- Reimaging social change. Let us take a look.

"Shared value is not social responsibility, philanthropy, or sustainability, but a new way for companies to achieve economic success." Michael E. Porter and Mark Kramer, "Creating Shared Value," Harvard Business Review

Shared value is a management strategy in which companies find business opportunities in social problems. While philanthropy and CSR focus efforts focus on "giving back" or minimizing the harm business has on society, shared value focuses company leaders on maximizing the competitive value of solving social problems in new customers and markets, cost savings, talent retention, and more.

More companies are now building and rebuilding business models around social good, which sets them apart from the competition and augments their success. With the help of NGOs, governments, and other stakeholders, the business has the power of scale to create real change on monumental social problems.

This is creating shared value:

THREE LEVELS OF SHARED VALUE

What does shared value look like?

#1 **Reconceiving Products and Markets**

Meeting societal needs through products and addressing unserved or underserved customers

Novartis: To reach customers without health access in rural India, Novartis offers a portfolio of affordable and appropriate medicines tailored to common regional health issues, which is increasing regional sales and doctor visits.

#2 Redefining Productivity in the Value Chain

Changing practices in the value chain to drive productivity through better-utilizing resources, employees, and business partners

Walmart: By reducing packaging and improving delivery logistics, Walmart saved $200M in distribution costs while growing the quantities being shipped. Purchase HBS Case Study

#3 Enabling Local Cluster Development

Improving the available skills, supplier base, and supporting institutions in the communities where a company operates to boost productivity, innovation, and growth

Chevron: To build prosperity in the region and improve its operating environment, Chevron's "Partner Initiatives in the Niger Delta" uses a data-driven approach to identify new market opportunities and local solutions to unemployment in the region.

THE SHARED VALUE JOURNEY

Where do you fall on the spectrum? We've found that companies just beginning their journey and companies who have been creating shared value for years require different resources and support. Read through the following, discern which you most resemble, and follow the resources you need to get started or continue at your level.

BEGINNER:

You're practising corporate philanthropy or CSR efforts that you're interested in taking to the next level with more strategic, business-focused efforts.

You need: More convincing that the shared value approach is the right approach for you.

ON YOUR WAY:

You're hard at work forming a shared value strategy, finding the right partners, and making the business case to corporate leadership and other stakeholders.

You need Practical how-to information to break down internal barriers and move shared value forward in your organization.

ADVANCED:

Congratulations! You have advocacy from leadership, you've reconceived your business model around a social issue, and now you're implementing shared value approaches at either the initiative or enterprise level.

You need the Inspiration to keep social innovation going strong and resources to scale up your efforts even more.

The most corporation will have to embrace the new order and discontinue CSR. It is however interesting we look for other means of impacting on people and organizations.

Let us look at the FrieslandCampina Hong Kong case study, sustained tradition and turned it into profits. This is an example of Shared value.

Case Study

FrieslandCampina Hong Kong: Keeping Traditions with a Visionary Approach

Over the past several years, FrieslandCampina (Hong Kong) Limited ("FCHK"), a subsidiary of Royal FrieslandCampina, has been taking major steps to preserve and enhance a vital aspect of Hong Kong's culture via a series of expansive initiatives that have long-lasting, rewarding outcomes. These initiatives have helped to fulfil local dreams via new job opportunities, boosted confidence amongst various sectors of the community and enabled cherished traditions to continue amongst a new generation, with one of the main goals being that a unique city tradition will carry on well into the future.

Much ado about Hong Kong-style Milk Tea

Cha chaan tengs, Hong Kong's version of local cafés, have been an integral part of the city's culture since the 1940s. Created as an inexpensive, filling, fast-paced hybrid of local and Western cuisines, the no-frills venues are

now an integral part of the city's daily life and collective memory. They've also been responsible for a unique "only in Hong Kong" food culture that has evolved over generations, involving highly specialised techniques requiring training and know-how.

One of the core components of this cuisine is Hong Kong-style milk tea, which has been recognised as one of the 20 items that are officially on the first-ever Representative List of Intangible Cultural Heritage of Hong Kong. A twist on British tea drinking traditions, the style that began in the 1940s is made from a mixture of different black teas using methods that vary at different cha chaan tengs.

But it's usually always mixed with one kind of evaporated milk: BLACK & WHITE®, the ubiquitous, nearly 80-year-old FrieslandCampina brand made of 100% fresh milk from the Netherlands. According to the South China Morning Post, it's estimated that at one citywide cha chaan teng chain alone, more than 10,000 cups of Hong Kong-style milk tea are made daily.

Yet due to a variety of factors, cha chaan teng culture and traditions have been on the decline over the last several years. These reasons include a lack of formal on-the-job training programme at many venues. Such venues offer specialised cuisine and techniques that elder generations can't pass to a new generation due to a lack of time, resources and impending retirement. There's also the realistic, everyday aspect of the cafés' relentless, bustling pace, which prevents potential new hires from being taken into the fold.

And, in the case of Hong Kong-style milk tea itself, the drink requires special training — similar to a good barista at a coffee shop — to create a satisfying drink for customers which is unique to Hong Kong. All of the above means that dedicated time and training is needed so that would-be employees can handle the daily aspects of the job with speed, competence and know-how. Without a formal succession programme, this is rarely happening today.

As a result, there have been fears that the traditions and techniques used to prepare such foods — especially Hong Kong-style milk tea — will be lost. In a bid to preserve what can be recognised as a highly specialised art form, FCHK has embarked on a series of initiatives.

The Milk Tea Master Training Programme

In Hong Kong, the company has teamed up with NGOs, a chef management school, and several restaurant groups to create a formal "New Generation Milk Tea Master Training Programme" every year since 2016. In 2018, organisations involved include the Hong Kong Confederation of Trade Unions Training Center, Baptist Oi Kwan Social Service, Evangelical Lutheran Church Social Service – Hong Kong ("ELCSS-HK"), Hong Kong Women Development Association and Urban Peacemaker Evangelistic Fellowship, as well as Star Chef Management School, Tai Hing Catering Group, Chrisly Café and Swiss Café. The programme was started in 2016 to prevent the technique from dying out and to bring new, qualified talent to the industry. In 2018, nearly 30 unemployed Hong Kong citizens (aged 18-59) each received 35 hours' worth of training that involved bar operations, food safety and techniques. 75 per cent of those who took part were then offered a 150-hour internship at a real cha chaan teng where they could receive much needed, fast-paced restaurant experience.

In an extension of the programme to pass on this culture and craftsmanship to the next generation, 20 students from a local secondary school were also selected to formally learn about Hong Kong-style milk tea making techniques and career skills in conjunction with the Youth Career Development Service of ELCSS-HK. The owner of Chrisly Café also provided entrepreneurial advice to students.

At the end of their training, the students were able to put their new knowledge to use via BLACK & WHITE® Milkteafé, a ten-day pop-up store held by the company in celebration of the 6thMilk Tea Day at Causeway Bay in November 2018. Two teams of students competed to sell the most BLACK & WHITE® combo sets over the course of a weekend. This provided them with much needed entrepreneurial and specialised Hong Kong-style milk tea training, and most importantly, enriched their lives with the opportunity to explore their interests and career aspirations. All proceeds from the event benefitted elderly service development to acknowledge the elderly's contributions to society.

Results

There have been several tangible short- and long-term results generated from FCHK's Hong Kong-style milk tea master training programme. First, the training programme has equipped the needy and unemployed with vocational skills to re-join the job market. The selected trainees themselves were offered a salary and letters of employment after completing their internship. Three of the interns were subsequently offered full-time employment at the cha chaan tengs that they interned with. To date, FCHK has trained nearly 150 professional Hong Kong-style milk tea masters.

All students, meanwhile, gained real-life entrepreneurial skills as two teams competed against one another in terms of selling BLACK & WHITE® combos that included Hong Kong-style milk tea made on-site. One student claimed that "the biggest challenge in making milk tea was time management and this programme gave me a practical opportunity to face society." One intern who graduated mentioned that the programme "allowed me to fulfil my dream," while others were grateful for both the opportunities presented and the recognition that they now have a "commitment to passing on this intangible cultural heritage of Hong Kong to the next generation."

That commitment to passing on this valuable cultural heritage may ultimately offer the biggest benefits for both Hong Kong and FCHK. With so many older milk tea "masters" retiring, the skills acquired by ongoing new trainees will enable the cha chaan tengs — and their traditions — to continue well into the future. It also ensures that it's being done the right way, both in terms of food safety and knowledge about how the business aspects of such venues work.

In the long term, such initiatives successfully keep the BLACK & WHITE® brand in the public eye. Currently, BLACK & WHITE® is the most used evaporated milk brand in nearly 80% of the cha chaan tengs in Hong Kong, based on a study conducted by Nielsen in December 2017 on "Brands in Evaporated Milk Category" among cha chaan tengs in Hong Kong. Such a figure helps BLACK & WHITE® maintain its number one share in the evaporated milk segment amongst its market base. The 79-year-old brand is also used in four out of every five cha chaan teng venues in the city.

As newcomers learn that the fragrance, texture and effect of the brand's use make for a better Hong Kong-style milk tea, the company is also creating the impression that its high quality is associated with good food service. In doing so,

BLACK & WHITE® becomes the brand to use at public venues and in the home. Associated promotions, such as the internship programme and an annual public "Hong Kong Milk Tea Day", help make BLACK & WHITE® evaporated milk the premiere must-have item in the category.

By supporting its customers and building capacity in the ecosystem – considered to be a cluster development approach, in shared value terms – demand for the BLACK & WHITE® products is perpetuated. Instead of moving only through traditional channels via wholesalers and distributors, this Training Programme creates and builds vital business-to-consumer relationships that extend to public cafés, such as cha chaan tengs and ultimately, daily consumers. As a result, brand recognition increases even more, and that recognition becomes associated with quality. Once that association has been made, customer loyalty — as seen by the recent Nielsen report — ensues.

While brand loyalty has been one result, regional public recognition has been another. Recently, FrieslandCampina Hong Kong was named the winner of two awards at the 10th Asia Responsible Enterprise Awards, which honours Asian businesses for championing responsible and sustainable business practices. This included an award for "Social Empowerment", as the company was selected from amongst 200 entrants across 14 countries.

As FCHK is seeing a relationship between its public programmes, its community engagement and ensuing results, their initiatives are expected to broaden and continue well into the future. What started as an initiative to help a sector of the community, has enabled a company to see lasting, sustainable results. "Moving forward, we will keep our commitment on nourishing the lives of Hong Kong people across all ages," says Natalie Yuen, Associate Director, Corporate Affairs of FrieslandCampina Hong Kong.

That commitment has proved to be more than nourishing. In the case of the New Generation Milk Tea Master Training Programme, it's also offering much-needed work to those who need it, educating future young employees about entrepreneurial skills and helping to ensure that an important aspect of Hong Kong society – in this case unique cha chaan tengs – thrives well into the future. That's good for Hong Kong, and it's proven to be extremely beneficial for FCHK.

This is an example of Shared value and this was executed by FrieslandCampina (Hong Kong) Limited and this led to the preservation of milk tea culture, collaborated with café's, restaurants to formulate a training program concerning Milk tea Master programme, this provided training for the unemployed, Jobs were created directly and indirectly at this locality, nourishing the lives of Hong Kong people across all ages and above all FCHK made more income because of this concept which has replaced CSR.

I want to advise our corporate bodies to embrace this concept because you must give back to the society and this would have a positive effect on our cooperation, I was privy to watching the interview granted by the Richest man in Africa to Mo Ibrahim an Ivorian Journalist, Aliko Dangote did mention that the west African market didn't allow him to sell his cement and within me, I realised that he should think of what he can give such societies in return when he makes another attempt to break into these markets, possibly could embark on shared value initiatives in that environment.

The soccer religion is all about love, unity and oneness, these traits should be evident in our lives as individuals, corporate entities, Governments at all level. A further look at the ecosystem of soccer you will realize that all components have a sole aim which is victory, I know you might wonder the composition of the so-called component, they are as follows: Players,

Coaching crew, Fans. Though there is an emotional connection of these three and the sole aim is always to win.

As a nation, we can achieve our set goals if we can come together as one and this has lots of positive implications. One of our challenges is selfishness, greed, lack of patriotism etc. Adapting this religion will help us in diverse ways. A politician should understand that he is a servant and desist from enriching him/herself by looting public funds, if we love our country then making positive impacts for the people, we represent will be our sole aim.

Have you considered the fact that a soccer team might be down and you see the fans have hope that there can be a turn around no matter what the situation looks like, FAITH binds this follower together and they continue to support their team and suddenly there's a spark, sudden improvements begin and before the regulation time success is attained?

We need not lose hope in our nation, with creativity on the path of our Leaders there will be total recovery. Making derogatory comments won't take us anywhere but ensuring we all contribute our little quota as individuals, corporate bodies will make us experience the improvements that we all expect.

There are times when a team will lose a match, the coach and his crew will go back to the drawing board to fix the challenges and afterwards, improvements will be noticed. As a nation we need to re-strategize, most times politicians make suggestions that will favour them, in the last constitutional conference, creating 18 additional states, Rotational presidency was on the agenda and today we here of restructuring i.e. a drift from federal governance to Regional governance and my simple question is that all these suggestions are from the same politicians, how patriotic are they concerning these suggestions.

I want to find out if these ideas are just for them to improve their chances of looting public funds or improving lives of a common man on the street, this should be the primary focus, do they have data to back up their claims concerning Restructuring and when we probe further we will realize that some ethnic groups might feel that they are marginalized and want to taste power.

www.ingramcontent.com/pod-product-compliance
Lightning Source LLC
Chambersburg PA
CBHW021935040426
42448CB00008B/1077